Witness Me

Witnessing the Supernatural Gifts of our Creator

Witness Me

© 2025 Darlene Marie
ISBN 9781896213132
Published by By Design Media, Paris ON CAN

All rights reserved. No part of this publication may be reproduced, stored in a retrieval system, or transmitted in any form or by any means without prior permission of the copyright owner.

Table of Contents

Introduction — 5
- My calling
- Demonic forces attaching themselves to our children
- The Holy Names
- A blessed mom

Chapter 1 *Boston* — 15
- Marrying YAHSHUA (JESUS)
- Standing in front of YAHSHUA
- The missing Virgin
- Dream visions
- A haunted house
- Perhaps a poltergeist
- My death experience
- The gift of hearing

Chapter 2 *Puerto Rico* — 31
- Low negative energy
- The gift of love
- Leaving a lesbian relationship

Chapter 3 *Europe* — 35
- Back from the dead
- The spirit realm

Chapter 4 *California* — 41
- The guiding dogs
- The Crash
- Time to leave

Chapter 5 *Cabo San Lucas* — 47
Time to heal
Rock people
Three devil masks
Cocaine in the field
First removal of a demon
Following my sewing machine in a vision
Serial rapist
The witch
The blood bank

Chapter 6 *San Miguel Allende* — 79
From drunk to His glory
An angel delivering Dene's name
Another vision of Mary
Father's money
Cleansing the house
Vision of an armored soldier
My repentance
Receiving the Torah in my heart
More possessions
Three dark angels
The Battle
Hearing, "Write the book, 'Witness Me'"

Chapter 7 *Suffer the Little Children* — 101
Suffer the little children
Living in CHRIST

Epilogue — 107
"But to all who did receive Him, who believed in His Name, He gave the right to become children of God." John 1:12

Prayer of Azariah — 109

Dedication

*I dedicate this to my
FATHER YAHUWAH
for it is He who gifted
me with these experiences
and told me to be a witness
of His supernatural gifts.
Amen*

*"This is the covenant that I will make
with them after those days,
saith the Lord.
I will put my laws into their hearts,
and in their minds will I write them..."*

Hebrews 10:16

Introduction

From my early childhood years, I was able to see angel beings and experienced other realms of reality. I often heard GOD talking to me, and experienced entering another dimension. When I would tell my mom about these things, she would always say, "Yes, I know, but shhhh, don't tell other people because they will come and take you away. Away; they will come to take you 'away.'" I never wanted to be taken "away," so I would talk only to my mom about these supernatural experiences.

I started writing things down, here and there through my life, as they happened. As the years went by, I gradually accumulated a stack of journals chronicling the somewhat winding, circuitous path of my life's journey – the raw material for this book.

My Calling

I know, now, that my calling has always been to walk with YAHUWAH. I believe His plan for my life right now is to bring awareness of the spiritual dimension in all of life, and to help people to deal with it effectively. For instance, it is critical for parents to know, as they raise their children, that the struggles of their lives do not always stem from what seems apparent. To be able to deal with their challenges with children and other members of their family, they need to be able to recognize the role played by spiritual entities in issues like child sexual abuse, among other things.

Having had to deal with a child who was molested from a very early age, I have become all too acquainted with the demonic entities that entered this child and others. I'll share more about this after I've shared how FATHER YAHUWAH guided my life up to the time when I would have to deal with these issues.

Demonic forces attaching themselves to our children

My purpose is to educate parents on the reality of demonic forces that interfere in the lives of children during times of trauma. Parents may try all kinds of things – like therapy – to "fix" them, but unless they deal with the dark spirits, they have no hope of getting to the root of their problems. Parents need to know how to go deep in the HOLY SPIRIT to bring their children through to freedom. This book will demonstrate how I was able to do so because of my dedication to FATHER. His hand has always been on my life, molding me to be an earthly vessel holding His HOLY SPIRIT.

The Holy Names

Just to back up a bit, I need to explain the terms I use to refer to "GOD" and "JESUS." Along the way, I discovered that He wants to be called by His rightful name which has been lost in general use for generations. About 50 years after the Resurrection, the Jewish rabbis started thinking about the effect His Name, as written in the original Hebrew text, would have on readers of Scripture. After all, they did not believe YAHSHUA (JESUS) was the MESSIAH. The problem was that in the Hebrew language, every letter has a meaning, and the word that is now translated in our Bibles as "GOD," was "Yod He Vav He," meaning, "The hand behold the nail behold." How much clearer could it be that YAHSHUA was the MESSIAH?

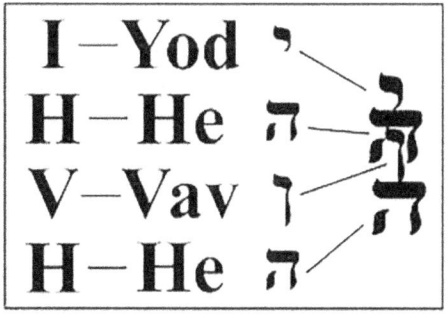

The Hebrew characters representing Yahshua arranged in a vertical column to show the similarity to the human body.

Oi vey. The rabbis solution was to tell the people that YAHUWAH's (GOD'S) Name was too holy to say. They claimed it would be blasphemous to speak it, and changed His Name to "ADONAI," translated from Hebrew to English as "GOD." The thing a lot of people don't clue in on, is that people were saying the Name "YAHUWAH" in the days of Moses. Was it not holy then? Most people refer to the SON of YAHUWAH as "JESUS," but JESUS means "Joshua." His Name is "YAHSHUA," meaning "salvation."

That is why I call FATHER "YAHUWAH" and His SON "YAHSHUA." I disagree with the rabbis.

A Blessed Mom

My mother gave me a strong faith in what she knew. She would sit on my bed at night and some mornings, and tell me that YAHSHUA (who we called "JESUS" at that time) was a man who loved everyone, fed the hungry, and healed the sick.

I wanted to be just like YAHSHUA. I prayed, "Please FATHER, bless me to be just like YAHSHUA so I may serve You."

As you can see, I started out with a solid foundation. That foundation was monumentally important in my ability to navigate the winding path through the situations and philosophies that later tried to destroy me.

My mother used to close her eyes and stand silently whenever she needed FATHER'S HOLY SPIRIT breath to fill her. I remember her doing this particularly at times when she would get angry or out of control, yelling at us kids.

She taught me to enter into the presence of YAHSHUA, and to know He was always there waiting for me. His temple was a space within my heart where I always wanted to be in His presence.

Scripture tells us we are to teach our young. Now I understand why. To fulfill YAHUWAH's purpose for my life, I needed a firm foundation to be able to survive the depths of the spiritual realm I would have to experience. I needed first-hand knowledge of spiritual realities, both light and darkness, so that He would be able to use me to remove demons from people, objects and situations. We are whole when we know FATHER YAHUWAH.

As I gradually grew into a solid relationship with the RUACH, the HOLY SPIRIT of the Most High, He guided me into a life of healing, seeing and extracting demons stuck in human bodies. It was not *me* doing any of these things; they would just happen whenever the SPIRIT opened the doors for whatever He wanted to do in people's lives. He taught me through the experiences He gave me.

I have always known, and trusted without doubting, that the anointed CHRIST dwells deep in my heart. He was, and is, always with me. He has always been my partner. Sometimes people question why I say "we" or "us," when they can see only me.

What an incredible ride! I am sometimes baffled at the gifts He shares with me. I am most grateful, and am always thankful.

My purpose in writing this book is to share this incredible journey as a witness of the many supernatural gifts He has given to equip me for His work among His people. I shall start with some of my earliest recollections and work up to the most exciting parts of this journey called "life."

This is not an ordinary, orthodox, religious kind of story. While I started life with my mother teaching me about YAHSHUA, I was not grounded in the Word of GOD. I didn't know His Word or His ways, but I *did* know that He was always with me. Sadly, because I wasn't grounded, I didn't understand the difference between New Age philosophies, false religions and authentic Christianity. I thought everything mystical was cool.

Far from being a saint, I stumbled through the years until my seventies, when I finally understood what needed to happen before I could truly align myself with the one true GOD, YAHUWAH.

Rather than write in some 'religious way,' I have included many experiences where I was stumbling, in hopes that anyone experiences some of the same things will recognize that they're off track and seek GOD to find how to align themselves with His true SPIRIT. I came to recognize my stumblings as lessons, as I grew in Him.

I was with FATHER YAHUWAH almost every night before I slept, and whenever I was in need. All I had to do was call on Him deep within my soul. Even though I strayed far from His ways on my journey, He never left me. I prayed and He listened. He always answered – but not always in the ways I expected. He was always there as I kept knocking on His door.

This book is about witnessing the reality of YAHUWAH. Without His RUACH (HOLY SPIRIT) guiding me, none of the following experiences would have happened. Most of them didn't even make sense to me until years later when, in deeper prayer, I understood what I was being shown.

I needed to sit quietly and listen before ABBA FATHER could send the RUACH to unwrap the lessons that He had prepared for me. Just recently, in prayer, I heard Him say, "Write the book, '*Witness Me*,'" and so here it is.

CHAPTER 1

Boston

Marrying Yahshua at the Age of Seven

I was around seven-years-old, and living in my birth city of Boston, when I had a dream that I married YAHSHUA, JESUS the CHRIST. The experience was very vivid. He gave me a wedding band. I awoke from the dream knowing nothing about the "Bride" written about in Scripture. It wasn't until about 60 years later that I learned about the Bride of CHRIST.

At the time of the dream, I felt quite guilty and ashamed. It felt blasphemous, even though I didn't even know the meaning of that word at the time. I buried the dream far back in my mind until it came up again years later. I don't even know if I told my mom when I had it, because I felt that I had sinned.

Standing in Front of Yahshua

On another day, between seven and 10-years-old, the nuns took us to see a movie of the CHRIST story. My love for Him was so deep that, when the soldiers took Him and nailed Him to the Cross, I was devastated. I felt as though I was there, standing in my body, witnessing this abomination of cruelty beyond any kind of imagination. I was having my first real-time spiritual experience…beyond my normal life-experience of beauty and love. I felt the deep pain of inconceivable injustice. I couldn't stop crying. A deep depression, rooted in inconsolable loss, began to overtake me. I was saddened to the point of being so deep in this torturous loss that I cried uncontrollably after the movie – until I was slapped across the face by a nun, slapped so hard that I saw stars. She stood over me, pulling me out and away from my sense of being right in front of CHRIST'S broken body. Many years later, as a woman was praying for me, she said, "I see a nun, two of them. One is saying she is sorry and that she repented for what she did." I could never understand why the nun didn't hold me and rock me through the spiritual experience, instead of smacking me.

I remember the pagan "May Poles" the nuns made the children prance around in springtime. They told us we were to hold onto the colored ribbons hanging from the tall pole and skip around in a circle singing. Some of the nuns were mean-spirited. If you didn't do what they told you, you got hit on the back of the hand on the knuckles with the metal part of the ruler, or you got your ponytail pulled. Sometimes they would slap you across the face to show who was boss. Then they'd lock you in a dark closet or sit you in a corner with your back facing the class.

Back then, I thought the way to be married to YAHSHUA was by being a nun. My love for YAHSHUA never failed, but my desire to be a nun was fading.

I was blinded and lacking in understanding. Nowhere in Scripture does it say you have to be a nun to be part of the Bride of CHRIST. I know that now, but it was confusing as a child.

The Missing Virgin

When I was around 10-years-old, my mother took a picture of me standing beside a Virgin Mary statue in the playground of the Catholic school I was attending. When the picture was developed, it showed me alone; the Virgin didn't show up in the photo. It was as though the statue was never there to begin with. You could see straight through to the street on the other side, all the way to the parked cars. My mom's family talked about this missing Virgin photo as if it was a big thing. That's why my memory of it is so clear. I grew up praying to the Virgin like all the Catholics, until I found out that Scripture tells us to honor FATHER through the SON. It says nothing about praying through the Virgin.

I had a few experiences years later in visions with the Virgin which I'll share when we get there.

Dream Visions

From the time I was seven or eight until I was around 13, I had a series of dreams that lasted for six years. For the first three of those years, the dreams were set in Egypt. For the next three years, the setting was in a city occupied by Roman citizens, perhaps Rome.

These dreams came to me in story-like dream-visions, always on or within the same three days in a row every year, as a continuation of the year before. They always began around the time of my birthday each year, give or take a day, depending on whether or not it was leap year. I have no idea why.

The first three-year set of dreams was always about a woman of royalty in Egypt. She looked like a queen all dressed in golden robes with straight, black hair. Bangs were cut straight across her forehead, just above the eyebrows. In every dream, she would walk into a room and sit on a pure gold throne decorated with deep blue lapis, on a raised gray, marble platform. This throne was the only furniture in the room. To the right of the throne were two dog-faced human-looking beings with pointed ears. It was as though they were half-dog and half-man, standing against the wall. I was under the impression that they had no voices.

The woman would always hold a mask of lapis and gold in front of her face and gaze at the sun through a narrow, oblong window in front of the throne. This sliver of a window was only about three or four inches wide, but it was very high. The room was small with a high ceiling. It was bright when the sunlight shone through this one window. The walls, floor and ceiling were all covered with highly polished, light gray granite or marble. I could almost feel and see the experience of the woman as if it were mine.

These first three yearly dreams were very similar; always with this same woman walking into this same room wearing royal, golden robes, going to the throne and sitting with the golden mask held up in front of her face as she stared, glaring at the sun as it passed by her view through the window.

Following the first series of three dreams, for the next three years on my next three birthdays, I had another series of three dream-visions. In this series, I saw the body of a small female clothed in silk veils that covered her legs and feet. I was under the impression that she had a veil around her face, although I never saw her face. Barefoot, she walked on tip-toe, moving quietly on dirt and cobblestone roads. I felt a great danger around her while she rushed, unnoticed, through the streets, hiding and ducking into the shadows of step-down openings before very old, massive wood-door houses, while passing by them. Was she a dancer? A slave? I don't know, but I could feel her fear. I would then see men and women in theatre-type arenas being put into dens to fight lions, and then being devoured by them as entertainment for a race of human beings indulging in hate crimes against humanity.

I recognized the streets and the voices in my dreams year after year. Every dream added to the last and became planted deeper in my subconscious.

Some of us children of YAHUWAH are gifted to see through our dreams and visions; sometime we can hear the RUACH talking to us. If we listen we can hear and make sense of them.

I believe these dreams were shadows of evil familiar spirits moving through the family lines of my ancestors. Familiar spirits are intimately acquainted with the people through whom they have lived and can be very successful in convincing people that they can connect with dead relatives or identify their own past lives. We must be careful not to succumb to Satan's traps. Pagans believe we have past-life experiences, as in reincarnation. This deception is another spin in the roaring lion's web of lies. Scripture says it is appointed unto man once to die and then the judgment comes. If it is appointed unto man to die only once, we cannot possibly have lived past lives. However, evil, familiar spirits that have entered the family line through some opening along the way through the generations can live through life after life in the family line, bringing intimate knowledge of ancestors with it.

Who was this Egyptian woman on the throne worshiping a false sun-god? Why did I see her for three birthdays in a row? Did she leave Egypt with Moses and the Israelites when they left captivity? Did successive generations become believers who underwent savage persecution under Roman rule?

Is it possible that the DNA passed down to us from our ancestors contains memories, experiences or gifts from the RUACH (HOLY SPIRIT)? If so, and if these are revealed to us by YAHUWAH, I'm sure He will have purpose in unfolding our understanding. Until then, it's a mystery.

One can only imagine, but our questions must always come back to the plumb-line of Scripture that tells us that it is appointed unto man once to die and then the judgment. If ABBA wants us to know or understand more deeply, He will reveal it.

The point is that we cannot make assumptions about things that we don't understand.

For now, I know that we have one body, one spirit, one lifetime. Only our ABBA FATHER and His BEN YAHSHUA have full knowledge about what our DNA holds. If we start digging around in things only He can know, it becomes a bottomless rabbit hole.

As I grew older, I was always confused about why others didn't know what I knew and see what I have seen. I couldn't understand why no one else talked about the love they had for YAHSHUA.

In order to see other realms, or beyond the veil, one must have a desire to experience life more deeply. By choice, one's faith becomes life in CHRIST, a knowing that He is always with us. That's how it was for me. I always walked with CHRIST by my side. I was never alone. We are connected through prayer. Without my connection to Him, I have nothing and am empty.

A Haunted House

When I was around the age of 12, we were living on the top floor of an older house, still in Boston. My mother was dating the man who lived on the bottom floor with his father. The story in the neighborhood was that his mother had been taken away because she saw the devil dancing on the roof in the pale moonlight. Being very young, I had no idea what that even meant.

In this house, I remember my mother reading the Bible at night at the kitchen table. Across from where she sat at the table, and above the kitchen stove, on the wall, there was a cross of light. I remember her changing the window coverings from shades, blinds and curtains to try to figure out what was causing the cross to appear, even when there was no moonlight. I remember hearing her tell her sister's family that the cross appeared only when the Bible was open on the table, or when it was in her hands as she sat at the table reading it.

This was a two-storey house with a basement. I remember being wakened some nights by something that sounded like chains being dragged across a floor. The sounds seemed to be coming from the basement where the old father would spend much of his time.

One night, I awoke to the sounds of water running. I jumped out of bed to check, and sure enough, there was a glass, half filled, in the sink under the faucet. I heard footsteps, so I went running into the hallway that led to the stairway leading down to the first floor landing. No one was there.

I walked down the stairs to where there were two doors; one led out to the street and the other, on the opposite side, behind me, went down to the basement. Both doors were locked from the inside. They were latched securely and bolted. No one could have disappeared from the hallway or from the stairway without walking through the walls. Had I been sleep walking? The footsteps had led directly to this hallway and there was no other room off the kitchen but this stairway. What was going on?

One might wonder how I could have been so brave as to investigate, but I never felt threatened or had fear. My sense of protection came naturally. It must have been FATHER'S wing covering me as in Psalm 91. I was always a brave child because I was aware of His protection being there, even though I never read about it until much later in life. Now I understand the "knowing." Through our prayers we can connect to YAHUWAH's divine power and His RUACH guidance within our mortal beings.

This may not be anything but words and meaningless experiences to some, and yet there is a window of time that calls those who are ready to hear. FATHER is calling us to know and experience Him.

Perhaps a Poltergeist?

During this time, I had a dog that I dearly loved. She was tragically killed by a car when I called her from across the street. As she came running to me, a car came from nowhere and ran over her. I heard a sound like a balloon breaking as the wheels crushed her to death. I cried for weeks without hardly eating. It was all my fault. My precious love was dead because of me. Sometimes at night while I was in bed after she died, I would feel an impression on the bed as if a dog jumped up onto the bed. I always thought it was the spirit of my dog coming to visit me. It seemed she would cuddle into the fold behind my legs as I went to sleep. This happened quite a few times with me always thinking it was her. Little did I know or understand that the trauma of her death could have opened the door to a disembodied spirit or some demon or fallen spirit. In those early days, I was unable to see this entity as I could in future times as ABBA opened my eyes to the spiritual forces around us.

We didn't last long in this house. Stranger things began to happen. One day my mother went screaming into the room that my baby brother was in. She was screaming about baby Butch being bitten by a snake in his crib. Sure enough, he had two puncture marks on his heel when my mom picked Him up out of the crib.

Then we began to hear that the woman of that house had been murdered and was buried in the cellar. Whether or not it was true, I may never know. It may have been nothing but a rumor. Nevertheless, there was something dark in that house.

My Death Experience

When I was around 13 to 14-years-old, I had to have an operation of some sort. After being put out with anesthesia, I could hear a bell ringing. I opened my eyes to see my body below me, lying on the operating table. The doctors were in chaos. I could see my mother sitting in another area, on the other side of a wall that I could now see through. She was stunned by the bell and a red light blinking above her head on the wall of the closed operating room where my body lay. I remember feeling sad for my mom – or maybe I was feeling her sadness. Whatever it was, it was a deep, deep sadness. I saw a machine that looked like a trash can with wires attached to it being wheeled down the hallway and into the room.

Then I saw everything that ever happened in my life flash in front of me. Like a fast-forwarding moving picture, it all ran together. My whole life flashed in front of me. Some of the scenes would stop so that I could feel the emotions of whatever came up in vibration and knowing. It always paused at anything I did that might have offended another human. Those scenes stayed longer than the flashing of other scenes. They were things like stealing my baby brother's bottle, withholding the truth from my mother, or trying to get rid of my kid sister for the day after my mom had given me strict instructions for watching her. There it was, my whole life flashing across my mind like a 3-D movie, with all the emotions that related to the pictures. Was I witnessing my judgment?

Then I was propelled up through the center of a tunnel towards a beautiful light ahead. It was brighter than anything I had ever seen before, or anything that I could put into words. I was utterly filled with love in this space. As I stood in front of the light, the question, "What did you learn?" was communicated to me in a vibration without voice or noise. It was just a knowing of what was being asked. And then I returned to my body, even though I wanted to be back in that place of love and light.

Throughout all the years following this experience, I have thought I was to learn something more. Now over 60 years later, in writing this and asking for truth, I understand the message. Love, obey and honor your parents, don't lie and don't steal.

Did I listen? Well, if I had learned everything I needed to know, I would never have become friends with my brother's ex-girlfriend who, in later years, tried to steal my soul. My mother warned me that Nealie was a witch, but I thought Mom was just plain crazy at times. Little did I know back then, that I still had much to learn to be able to navigate this life without harm from the dark side.

I was blessed beyond words with this near-death experience. My heart is so full, and I cry at times because YAHSHUA loves me enough to share wonderful experiences and gifts like this with me. When I pause and meditate on His goodness, I become overwhelmed. At times, I am unable to find words to express the fullness of my heart because of all the gifts He has given me.

The Gift of Hearing

I was born legally deaf, but was gifted with an operation when I was about 13. It involved the transplant of a lamb's eardrum. My own eardrum had been perforated. Over the years, the hole was getting bigger, and what hearing I did have was rapidly deteriorating. I was having increasingly painful earaches. Oh, the pain, crying and screaming. At least once or twice a week, my mother would take me to the Massachusetts General hospital in a little red wagon. My hospital book was full of sheets of paper, each recording a visit. I was chosen for the transplant because of this book being so full. When I first met with the transplant doctor, he said he expected a very old person because of all my hospital visits. I know that FATHER had His hand on this.

The operation was performed without cost to us by Doctor Gross, who traveled all the way from Germany. I understand it was a nine-hour operation performed under a microscope, and involved a few weeks of sitting by an uncovered light bulb for a few hours everyday, drying up the liquid to heal the wound.

When they removed the bandages, I could hear sounds that I had never heard before. What a gift! Hearing the rain on the windows and the songs of the birds was a true delight. Again grateful, I was always taken care of and always aware of my guiding, guarding angel. Thank you, FATHER. Thank you.

CHAPTER 2

Puerto Rico

Low Negative Energy

When I was about 24-years-old, I went on vacation to Puerto Rico with a live-in lover and a few friends. After they left, I stayed and got a job.

I was on a beach, sun-bathing one day in late fall. There was no one to be seen on the beach. The native people would never go to the beaches in winter, from late October to springtime. I was alone – or so I thought, until I felt a low, negative energy. As I looked around, I spotted a man about 15 feet from me, hiding in a bush. He was sitting there, masturbating. I pick up a rock and threw it hard, hitting the target. He got up and started to chase me. He was very angry. I knew that if he caught up with me, with no one around, I was in grave danger. I ran away from him on the beach, waving at the boats that were far out in the water as I ran, hoping that this man chasing me would think I was being watched.

That didn't work. He continued chasing me. Way up in front of me, I could see something or someone. I ran towards this figure, all the time praying for help. The closer I got, the more distress I communicated to the figure ahead. As I got closer, I could see it was a Doberman dog. She was jumping up and down with a puppy beside her. When I got to the dog and her pup, I collapsed, crying. She took off chasing the man, who I never saw again. I knew I had spiritual help guiding the whole situation.

I am blessed and grateful for all the protection ABBA FATHER has given me over all these years.

The Gift of Love

I truly believe it is important to be grateful all the time. FATHER knows our hearts, and being grateful generates good vibrations that fill the atmosphere around us with loving energy and attract a loving response from those around us.

Leaving a Lesbian Relationship

Still in Puerto Rico, I met a man, Mick, with whom I began to spend significant time. I was tending bar at Helga's where he and his friends hung out. It was the neighborhood dump with hardly any business at all; but for me, it was an income.

After awhile, I quite my job and moved in with Mick. He worked for Crowley Maritime, a company based in Seattle WA. The company moved shipping containers, pipeline, and other things on tug boats and barges around the world. We were having a great time, when Mick was called to go overseas for a new job in Antwerp. When he suggested I should go with Him, I thought why not. I was in love. So I was off on another worldly trip, always grateful for what was put in front of me.

I remember Puerto Rico as the place I was gifted with a man who loved me and was willing to take me with Him. It was through Mick Watkins that I was able to forget a sinful, seven-year lesbian relationship in my birthplace of Boston. I never returned to Boston again, except to visit family. Did I feel GOD'S hand in this? Most definitely.

So off to Europe we went.

CHAPTER 3

Europe

Back From the Dead

Life wasn't as much fun in Europe as it had been on the beach. Our friends were different. They were more professional. We found ourselves spending less time together, but this didn't last long. Before we knew it, Mick got another transfer to Saudi Arabia. Before he was to leave, we planned to go to California to find a house for me. His folks had just moved to Alamo, California from Seattle Washington. His father was a senior executive with Crowley. We would visit them and find a home. Plans were in the making.

Mick did not want me to go to Saudi Arabia. He felt it was no place for an American woman. So we started packing.

A few weeks into packing for our new journey, life changed drastically. Mick and I were in a terrible car accident that took the life of my beloved.

Minutes before the impact, I bent down to change the cassette tape in the car and so did not see anything coming at us. This was when tape decks were bolted down under the front console. Suddenly, I felt a bunch of thumps and bangs which tossed me around. The car stopped. It was pitch black out. I noticed when I sat up, that Mick was not in the car. The soft top of the car had been torn off. We had been hit, head-on, by a truck carrying metal stagings for building large structures. Our small car, a 190 SL Mercedes-Benz convertible, had been shoved over against the guard rail. This accounted for the bumps I felt while hunched down under the dashboard. The impact broke one of the thick cords that held the giant staging rods on top of the truck. One metal L-shaped rod bumped its way down off the pile and through our front car window. As it ripped off the soft top, it tore through Mick's shirt, cutting his major vein and impaling him through his neck. Mick's body was pushed backwards. The rod went right out through to the other end of the car. Mick was then pushed forward through what was left of the windshield and projected out of the car. Terrified, I managed to get out, and I ran, searching for Mick, asking FATHER to help us. I was guided to his body laying in a pool of blood from his head down. I couldn't find the wound to hold it closed, because when he hit the ground, the shirt went back up covering his neck and the wound.

I was frantic. With all the blood, I knew we were in trouble. Mick was not making any noise until I told him he had to take CHRIST into his heart. Then I heard a moan, just before his body shook with the death rattle. I will never forget it. As I bent over his body on my knees, holding Him, I screamed that he could not leave me and asked GOD to please, PLEASE, **PLEASE** help us. I took Mick's face in my hands and put my mouth to his, attempting CPR. His body started breathing again. I had to take off my coat, now weighed heavy with blood as I laid in the puddle of his life, next to him. I hardly remember the ambulance taking us to the hospital. Even now, my heart cries big as I write and re-write these lines of heart-breaking devastation.

I remember sitting up, crying in a hospital bed, as the doctors, standing at the foot of the bed, told me they were giving Mick blood, but his liver was busted. His body was clearly not receiving the foreign blood as the doctors worked on Him. Two other doctors came in to reassure me that they were doing what they could to take out the glass that was embedded in his face and eyes, and filled me in on what was happening in the operating room. There were three of them working on Mick.

The Spirit Realm

After many hours, I had a strong sense that Mick's spirit was moving forward in death. I was given the understanding that his body would never be as it was and it would be difficult for Him to live like that. When all three doctors came and stood in front of my bed to break the news of Mick's death to me, I told them I already knew he had left. They were all baffled as to how I knew, and I told them I had been told in the spirit that he was leaving.

Mick's death was a massive trauma for me, one which took me home about a week later. The hospital had kept me on suicide watch because I was having a hard time. I couldn't eat, drink or sleep. All I could do was cry. My heart was broken, even though I knew Mick had accepted FATHER when we were on the ground.

The first night after leaving the hospital, I walked into a light-filled apartment. I thought it would be dark, but it was full of peace. I felt the warmth of Mick's body next to me when I lay down to sleep that night. I could smell his body on the sheets.

I had to pack up everything before I could leave to go on to start a new life – who knew where – but I had to bury Mick first.

Mick was buried in Seattle, Washington, where he was born.

Alan Michael Watkins,

Born December 10th, 1946; Died December 17th, 1976.

The service was held at the Floral Hills Funeral Home, January 3, 1977. At the funeral, I discovered that as Mick grew up, he had told everyone – except me – that he would never live past 30-years-old. The only way he ever got close to sharing that with me was by making me promise that I would play Bob Dillon's music (or have Dillon play) at his funeral, and he bought me a life insurance policy one month before his 30th birthday. It was easy to put all the pieces together after hearing all his friends talk about how Mick had known of his own death years before it happened. Did he wish it upon himself – or how did he know? His mom told me all Mick wanted was a woman to love and for her to love him back. He got his wish. Thank you, ABBA FATHER, for the gift.

I told his dad that the only thing Mick asked of me, concerning his death, was that he wanted to be in California and made me promise that I would have Dillon play at his funeral.

At the funeral in Seattle, Mick's body was in a closed casket at the funeral home, but the casket was placed empty in a plot in the ground where all his family and friends could visit. Mick's dad had Him cremated. Afterwards, his mom, dad and I went on to California, carrying his ashes. Mick's work company arranged a marine salute. As I tossed his ashes out over San Francisco Bay, there was no Dillon, but a grand group of fire tug-boats saluted with streams of water from their fire hoses out over the Bay. They saluted him right into ABBA's arms.

I decided that I would stay in California. That was where we had been planning to go; and so, carrying Mick in my heart, I did the best I could. Other than his Bible and our pictures, I gave everything away.

CHAPTER 4

California

The Guiding Dogs

California –land of rafting and camping, the things I liked best. In a highly memorable adventure, I went with some friends down the Truckee River on a two-day raft trip. The part of the river where we rafted had about 200-foot mountains on both sides. The only way out was down the river. The first day, I was bounced out of the raft and swam ashore. The other rafts in our party had already passed me. Here I was, standing on a tiny bit of sandy land with mountains on each side of me. Because the waters were so rough, it was impossible to swim over to the other side, and I couldn't climb over the mountains by foot. Looking around, I found a very narrow trail and began to follow it as best as I could. I thought someone must have done this before, leaving this trail behind. Still wearing my back pack, I continued to follow the trail. It led me deeper into a heavily forested area. Within steps into the unknown, it became more like a jungle.

All of a sudden, a pack of dogs came crawling up out of a large hole in the earth, heading right towards me. They were making it known that this was their backyard, and I was intruding. A female and four angry males all growled and hunched down as if to attack. They formed a circle around me and started jumping up and down as they walked round and round me. Calling on FATHER in my mind, I started spinning in a circle faster and faster in the opposite direction of their walk. I started to feel a peace and my mind filled with thoughts of feeding them. As I spun, I held tight to my back pack, swinging it off my back and stopping quickly, crashing it on the ground in front of me. I then said to them out loud, "I need your help and in return, I will feed you."

At this surprising turn of events, all the dogs stopped and sat in a circle around me. The female got up and went back into the hole, while the other four dogs formed a line in front of me. They started to walk further into the depths of the forest on this very narrow sort of trail. I followed them, knowing FATHER had sent an angel (a messenger) to orchestrate all this, because I had no fear. I had a knowing that they were going to get me out of this mess. Sure enough, they led me right to the water's edge. To my surprise, the rafters in my party were right there on the other side of the river, setting up camp. They had already started a fire. I crossed over this calmer part of the river to the other bank, went to the cooler and threw two packages of hamburger to the dogs on the other side, where they were sitting and waiting. It was amazing how protected I felt. Maybe this is what the armor of YAH feels like when one truly has been given the gift of faith. FATHER ELOHYM has always been there and I have always felt His strength in me.

The Crash

In 1979, California had a Savings and Loan crash that shut down the money system. All of a sudden, the interest rates went from nine percent to 21 percent, overnight. It was a disaster almost too unbelievable to be true. People lost everything they had saved, robbed by a few evil doers. Did anyone care? Not a minute. If they had, they would have given the money back to the people, but I don't think that happened.

I had always felt so protected by the HOLY SPIRIT in other areas of my life that I was largely naive to things happening around me. I paid no attention to the news or what was happening in the world. A war in Vietnam was being fought, but I was oblivious to it.

I had a feeling that YAHSHUA had different plans for me again. Money was not regularly coming in and banks were not lending, totally shutting down the world around me. Selling real estate was not a happening business at the time and so...again, I just walked away. After selling what I could of my personal belongings, and packing a duffel-bag of necessities, I dropped the keys at the front door, got on a bus and started another new life experience, leaving behind a four-plex, a condominium and a large home not far from a lake. The house backed onto 13 acres of land designated as non-buildable land. Because of this, what I would miss most were the deer that hung out in my back yard on the property.

Time to Leave

In October 1981 I made my way to Cabo San Lucas, Mexico, to heal and maybe write this book. I imagined that it would be a two-year sABBAtical, but it became more than that. I needed to feel the hot sun on my back and the sand between my toes. Now, here we are, 44 years later, still in Mexico, finally writing this book in *FATHER'S* time, not mine.

I journeyed down to Mexico with only necessities, running away from a bunch of friends who were all hooked on drugs. Unencumbered by worldly possessions, it was easy to travel. I just needed to heal from the losses, and to let go of the material world for awhile. I had a whopping $4,200 U.S. dollars to my name. With no fear or worries, I followed an inner knowing that all was going to work out. It always did. I thought I would find a job cooking on a boat while I sorted my years of experiences into writings to get over the pain of it all. I traveled by bus to Cabo San Lucas, stopping here and there along the way to do interviews for deck help jobs that had been posted in Southern California. I was 33 or 34-years-old.

I guess CREATOR YAHUWAH had to add more experiences to my journey; some of the best, some of the most interesting and some of the most hair-raising years of my life.

No matter what, I was always grateful.

CHAPTER 5

Cabo San Loucas

Time to Heal

I was learning that I don't belong in just one single spot on this planet as I journey home to my CREATOR.

After letting everything go into foreclosure and shutting the door on the previous part of my journey, it was time to heal from the losses and let go entirely of the material world.

I had YAHSHUA by my side. What else did I need? I had a duffel-bag of essentials, a small, hard-covered book about YAHUWAH, the Great I Am, and my mother's small Bible.

Putting a bunch of things in storage, I was off to Cabo San Lucas on the Baja peninsula. Wow, what a ride. I had no idea what would await me.

After having run away from my first job as a cook on a fishing boat, I was guided to the smallest rental in which I'd ever lived. It was just one tiny room, and it cost $50 a month. Yup, things were almost free in Mexico back in 1982. FATHER took very good care of me. I was gifted.

I lived practically free in a fabulous beach town. There was a handful of Americans living there, maybe two handfuls, counting the tourists (who stayed on from time to time) and those who lived on fishing boats. Occasionally I would meet people who came ashore for food. They were just passing through, living on sail boats, on their way to other spaces. I thought maybe I could get a job on one of those boats and travel on, but something held me back. I was getting used to living in a very small, confined room in the middle of nowhere's desert. For now, this was home away from wherever it was I was heading towards.

Cabo San Lucas, back then, was a sleepy, tiny Mexican town; clean, dusty and hot. There was one hotel in town – the Marti Cortes. The Finestera was on the point, at the end of town, where the Pacific meets with the Sea of Cortes.

Rock People of Cabo San Loucas – Carved Stone Mini Gods

I have a picture of the giant rocks on the point. They looked like larger-than-life rock people with eyes and noses, all with different faces and hairstyles. Some even appeared to have curly hair. Could these structures have been Watchers turned to petrified rock when they were destroyed by the flood? Or maybe they were carved stone, pagan mini gods. If you look closely enough, you can see giant stone fish rising up out of the sand. You can see the picture I took of them that I hardly showed to anyone until now.

It was time for me to deal with the pain of loss and to find a way to support myself.

Rock People of Cabo San Lucas

Mindfully walking through those days with my CREATOR, I spent more time in prayer and writing about how grateful I was, than reading the Bible.

Confused by the New Age deception in the 80s, I thought I could mix and mingle other belief systems. I had no understanding of pagan practices; Buddhism, and Yoga being deceptions of the dark side. A little here and a little there looked like truth to me, with lots of ways to Heaven. As long as the narrative included the buzz word of "love," it must be good. Ha-ha – deception at its best! Because I wasn't grounded in the Word, I was vulnerable to deception and to Satan, who was disguised as the angel of light.

Even though I was not on the straight and narrow path, FATHER always had His angels watching over me. I knew I was always protected. Whenever I entered a room or stood next to someone who was unclean, I could feel dark energy. I was very sensitive to the things of the spirit, although not skilled in discernment. I needed to be taught the ways of our CREATOR.

I wanted to be worthy and my gifts were many. I experienced a wonderful sense of freedom with visions and "knowings" (my word for divinely inspired intuition) that others could neither see nor understand.

I learned about the way we were created with energies and molecular vibrations, all the time staying in close contact with the HOLY SPIRIT, with whom I had learned to walk at a very young age. I confess to not always listening to His messages and guidance, but I always had a sense of being safe. I was still praying a lot and writing in journals about my gratitude to my CREATOR. By this time, I had a stack of these journals I'd filled, because life without the HOLY SPIRIT would have been boring, to say the least.

As I walked through these desert days, I grew in strength and healing. I began to learn to identify spirits of dark-side deception. Now I understand that FATHER was getting me ready for something bigger as He kept me under His wing of protection. I was still naive, (stupid if you really want to know), so the RUACH had to hit me with a bat over the head at times, in order for me to understand what He was trying to show me.

I prayed a lot, I played a lot and I grew a lot. In my tiny room, I learned to be an artist. After awhile, I opened a store to sell the jewelry and clothing I was making and trading.

One day I noticed a very handsome, but thin man who had moved into town. Noticing him made me think that the empty hole left after Mick's death must have been healing. Interesting. I learned that his name was Jose Louis and that he was the editor of the new, and only ever (that I knew of), newspaper in town.

Jose Louis's best buddy was the head of Immigration. After having lived in Cabo for a few years by now, I knew I needed to get legal. This gift of connection was put right in my lap. Getting my legal working FM-3 papers made it so much easier to sell my creations to the boutiques in big hotels in Mexico. Reporting to the government and paying taxes to this country fell into place. Being away from the country of my birth and staying much longer than planned, was becoming comfortable and, for me, home for now. When I learned that I still had to pay social security taxes in the USA, I shrugged my shoulders and decided to do my best to pay Caesar whatever belonged to Him.

When I started advertising in the newspaper, Jose asked me out to his favorite restaurant for dinner. There was a good piano player and nice soft music. Wining and dining, I guess they called it.

Three Devil Masks

One day, Jose Louis came to the store with a box full of Mexican devil dance masks. He said they were a gift and told me to put them on the walls and sell them. The man selling them had come over from the mainland and needed money, so Jose Louis had bought them for me. I would not accept this kind of gift, let alone hang them in my store. I didn't want them, no matter what the story behind them might have been. I knew some sort of darkness was attached to them. So I borrowed a friend's truck and took these three, very large, devil wood masks with me to a secluded beach. Finding the perfect spot, I put them face down in the box that they came in and lit them on fire. I said a prayer to YAH, worshiping Him for all

He is and giving eternal thanksgiving. As I prayed with eyes closed, I heard a big bang. The next thing I knew, the three masks were all face up and out of the box in a triangle position. All their faces were facing in the same direction. It freaked me out, so I let them burn where they were.

I got in the truck and started the engine. I put the truck in drive, but as it went forward, the tires dug a hole and got stuck. I put the engine into reverse, but the tires got deeper and deeper. They were buried in beach sand. Back and forth and back and forth I went, but I was really stuck. I turned to our CREATOR YAH and prayed. Then I got out of the truck to check the situation and noticed a rug in the back of the truck. How convenient! It was a fancy Asian rug, big enough to fit under the tires to give me traction. I was free in a grateful minute. To this day, Jose Louis has no idea that I borrowed the truck, took the masks to the deserted beach and burned them.

Cocaine in the Field

The devil never stops testing us.

The friend who owned the truck I borrowed told me he had some coke. It had been a handful of years since I'd done cocaine, so I gave in to temptation and thought I'd just do one line. Well, whatever it was, it blew the top of my head off. I could hear my life force escaping as if there was a hole in the top of my head, and out it was blowing! My heart was beating so fast I thought it was going to burst. I hit the john, sicker than a dog. Sitting there, I started to pray, "FATHER please help me! I promise…"

"I promise…" Don't we all do this? We run to Him whenever we are in need. But what about Him? Where is He? FATHER is always calling us…always. We just need to hear Him.

It took me a few days to get over that one line, but enough to make me promise to never do it again.

When I was strong enough to get up and out, I took a walk to the marina. On my way there, I passed through a big empty field. It was a beautiful day and I was grateful to be alive. In the middle of the field I was crossing, I raised my hands to FATHER YAH, and with my heart I told Him that I was so blessed to have Him and, stomping my foot, I promised I was done with coke. As I stomped my foot, a vial, half full of white powder, popped up out of the ground. Rather than bend down and pick it up, I started to bury it with my foot. As I was digging a hole to bury it, up popped another vial. As I started to stomp on them both, a third one was uncovered. Sometimes the truth is stranger than fiction. I was being tested. I stood there, knowing I had made a promise to my CREATOR, so I put my hands up to Him and told Him I was done. And I walked away.

First Demon Possession

Crazy things happened to me during this time of learning. Stuck in a crevice between light and darkness, I was still struggling to find my way.

On the 11th of February, 1986, there was a new moon. It was a brand new month. That day, FATHER used me to cast a demon out of the arm of a man I'll call Armandingo.

I had gone out for a drink to the Giggling Marlin. It was a big new bar and restaurant in town. Somehow I got talking to a complete stranger who introduced himself as Armandingo. He was very distressed and started telling me about his life. He showed me a scar in his arm that went from the middle of his wrist to the elbow on the outside of the arm. At the elbow part of the scar, there was a hole that was seeping a liquid.

He told me that he had been married, but that his wife and son had left him for a friend. He went on to say that several years ago, they had all gone together for a ponga ride. (A ponga is a little metal boat that holds up to five or six people.) While out at sea, a storm came upon them and capsized the boat. He claimed to have been the only survivor and woke up on the shore with a nasty cut on his arm. He had it stitched, but it never healed at the elbow.

After a few drinks, we went to my room, a slightly larger one-room space, to roll a joint. I remember sitting on the bottom edge of my bed with him standing and facing backwards in front of me, when I was overtaken by a sudden impulse to grab him and pull him on top of me backwards. My hold was amazingly strong as his arms and legs flailed, trying to get free. I felt like I was dreaming, What on earth was happening? I couldn't believe I was doing this to a stranger. All of a sudden, a voice came out of me; a very deep, strong voice that was not mine. It felt like a demanding roar as I heard myself saying, "I command you to come out in the Name of JESUS CHRIST. Come out of him now!"

Was that me? Definitely not.

The man's voice also changed. It was deep and angry. "Let go of me!" As he struggled, arm and legs kicking in a frenzy, still locked in a hold on top of me, he did his best to get free from the grip I had on him. The struggle didn't last more than a few minutes or so, when this deep, strong voice that didn't belong to me demanded again that the evil spirit in him had to come out in the Name of JESUS CHRIST. All of a sudden, a dark form came out of this man and went right up to the ceiling and out through a corner of the room, disappearing from sight. I relaxed my hold on his body. The man got up and, shocked, said, "What the f--- was that?"

Stunned, I said, "I don't know." He ran to the door and left. I never saw him again.

Life was surely getting very interesting for me. Every night, and sometimes for days, I would stay in prayer, fasting and writing thanksgivings to my ELOHYM, FATHER CREATOR YAHUWAH.

I still had no fear. Despite all of these strange things, nothing scared me. I was protected. My prayers every night connected me to a power greater than I. I was no angel, and nowhere close to deserving this protection. All I knew was that I loved YAHSHUA and my FATHER YAHUWAH. My life was empty without constant prayers of thanksgiving to them both.

Following my Sewing Machine in a Vision

Still living in Cabo San Lucas, I went to visit my mom in Boston.

I had just landed at the Boston airport carrying my sewing machine. I had purchased this sewing machine on monthly payments when I was around 13-years-old, and had stowed it under my airplane seat. I had paid for it with the allowance Mom gave me to wash the dishes and watch my sister and brother while she worked. This machine was my only tool, other than a pair of scissors and a tape-measure, for bringing in an income those days. By that time,

I was designing clothing for a living, having been gifted with the creative use of my hands by the grace of our CREATOR.

After the plane landed, I took my sewing machine to a spot by a phone-booth. It was one of the old-fashioned red ones that had a sliding glass door and a phone that accepted coins. I went to pick up my luggage from the conveyor belt and to look for Nealie, my brother's ex-girlfriend, who had come to pick me up. When I returned to the phone booth with Nealie (the one who my mother had warned me was a witch) where I had left the sewing-machine, it was gone.

I went quickly into the phone-booth, closed the doors, closed my eyes, put my hands up above my head and started praying for help. In a vision, I could see the bottom of a man's body, his pants just above his shoes and ankles, carrying my machine by his side. He was on an escalator staircase, going up the stairs as it moved electronically. I pushed the doors of the phone-booth open like super-girl and followed the vision. I was grateful for the angels that were guiding me. As I followed the scene in my head, I entered a room marked, "Lost and found," and there was my machine, sitting on the left-hand side of the room, on the floor, next to the door, exactly where my vision had showed me it would be. Praise YAH.

This kind of listening and knowing has been part of my life in so many amazing experiences. I honestly used to think everyone could see and do these things. It seemed so natural to me. I was always in prayer and always grateful.

Serial Rapist

Being grateful and prayerfully asking to be of service continually, I was gifted with the rental of a tiny A-frame house. Because Cabo San Lucas was so hot and desert dry, I left the front door open much of the time. One day, from where I was standing by the open door, I could see a young man staring at me as he walked in my direction. I went into the house to escape his glare, but he followed me right into the house and asked for water. I told him to leave and gave him water as he left.

A few days later, my car had scribbling on it by the mirrors. It looked like the doodling of a young school child.

November 3rd, 1986, I had just lain down to sleep when I was suddenly awakened by the weight of a body on top of me. When I opened my eyes, I realized a man had my shoulders pinned to the bed with his knees. He was sitting on me with a knife at my throat.

As I struggled to see if this was a dream, I immediately cried out silently to the Virgin Mary (another lesson was yet to come) to PLEASE tell me what to do. As I prayed for safety, I was guided into doing what I was told. I took off my clothing, but kept praying. I felt safe and everything was calm. As I prayed inwardly, I felt separated from my body which reacted in a way it never had before when having sex. Very strange feelings flooded over me and I was not hurt. My entire focus was deep in prayer. I was kept in a state of grace that was in total control of the situation.

After the man finished raping me, I had a strong sense that I was to draw his picture. I told him I was an artist and wanted to remember him by drawing his picture. In my mind, I was thinking that I would have it in the house for the police when I reported the rape. I found myself inviting him back for lunch the next day. He stuck the picture in his pocket before crawling out the same window through which he had entered the house. I was not good at drawing, but somehow I re-drew his likeness on a piece of paper, and that was why the police found the man guilty, and took him away.

Many years later, while praying to be of service again, I was struck with the realization that I had been given the chance to take a demon out of the serial rapist. Back then, I never even thought of it, even though it was just months after the HOLY SPIRIT had used me to take the demon out of Armandingo's arm. Here I was with a possessed schizophrenic and I hadn't been able to put it all together. I was still learning and not always getting it at almost 40 years old, but ABBA FATHER never gave up on me.

After the young man left, I broke down in deep sobs that enveloped my being. I forgot that I had an appointment with Jose Louis for dinner that night until he knocked on my door. I don't remember the time. Nothing mattered but dealing with what had just happened. When I answered the door, Jose Louis could see that I was stressed and asked what had happened. When I told Him, he took me to his apartment and called his buddy, the head of immigration, who in turn called the town's judge, who in turn arranged for me to go into the hospital and have a rape test. All this happened in the middle of the night. To my surprise, when the nurse was taking samples, I was full of blood – my blood. How was it that I never felt any pain? It wasn't my period. Something was strange. It didn't make sense. Had I been protected from the pain, or what was going on? Had this been done to show the police the truth through supernatural means?

I was at the hospital for hours. After the rape testing, I had to give my statement to the federal police through a translator. If I remember correctly, it was around 11 a.m. the next morning when the federal police drove me back to my place. As we drove up the road near my house, I saw the rapist walking toward us. When I told the officers, the one in the back seat jumped out of the open convertible jeep with his rifle pointed at him and arrested him. They found the picture that I told them I had drawn in his pocket, and my blood was all over his inside clothing. They put him behind bars immediately. A day later, the police came to me with questions about why I had undressed and allowed this man to have his way. I told them that I felt if I didn't, he would have killed me. I was saddened by all this because, despite what he had done to me, the boy was a 22-year-old schizophrenic and needed to be in some sort of care, rather than in jail.

At the time, I was not yet sufficiently awake to see FATHER'S plan in this. Sometimes I needed to be hit with an experience so shaking that I could see what the FATHER was trying to tell me.

About 10 days later, the police came knocking on my door to tell me that I had done Mexico a great service by reporting all this as soon as it happened. Apparently this man had raped another 10 young girls on his way down the Baja peninsula, stopping in different towns on his way to Cabo San Lucas by bus. Only FATHER knew how many others were hurt by the monster that possessed this young man.

Now, just now, many years later, because of other experiences I have since had, I am able to see this story in a different light. This man had to be stopped. I believe I was chosen to stop him. It is ABBA's story to other believers and those coming to Him after all these years. I asked for this. After all, I prayed almost every night asking to be used. At that time, the night this all happened, because I did not understand, I told FATHER that I didn't want to be used anymore, that this was way too difficult and that putting a young man in jail was hard.

At the time, I didn't realize that maybe this boy had been a victim himself, as so many in our world today have been. He could have been a victim of pedophilia. Dark spirits use our children and mess them up so badly that their minds fracture, enabling demons to possess their bodies. I'll say more about this later.

I was able to forget about this young man until what I supposed would be the timeline for him to be freed and possibly out looking for me.

This little desert beach town was changing surprisingly fast. Big name hotels started going up all along the coast.

As I write this, a dove sits on the tree right outside my office window. I believe it as another reminder that YAH is always with me and shows me the way.

Nealie - The Witch

What happened next was not an accident. YAHSHUA was in charge and I was about to be shaken like never before. I was to have an experience which took me years to process and figure out what the heck really happened. It was all part of the process of being awakened to the understanding of how the HOLY SPIRIT works in us.

New age stuff was popping up all over the place in the 1980's and I was trying to figure it all out. Despite my Christian heritage with my mom being a very Godly woman, my experiences of ABBA FATHER protecting me, and my deep gratitude when sensing the presence of YAHSHUA or our HOLY SPIRIT, the RUACH, I was vulnerable because I wasn't grounded in the Word of YAHUWAH. I had read bits and pieces of the Bible but certainly not enough to be able to discern light from darkness. In those days, I would open the Bible at random and read some Scripture, but never the whole book – yet.

My brother's ex-girlfriend, Nealie, told me she was a "pagan." I had never heard of a pagan before and had no idea what that was or what it meant at the time.

In total naiveté, I was about to embark on a major demon possession encounter with Nealie. It was another of many that were to follow. Through the experience, years later, I was able to develop the strength that GOD brought me to understand.

My mom never liked me hanging with Nealie, especially when I went to visit her. She would tell me Nealie was not of our GOD. Nevertheless, Mom bought pearls for us both. I still, to this day, have mine – but Nealie buried her necklace in the back yard. She knew my mother was a Godly woman and she disliked her as much as my mother disliked Nealie, maybe even more. FATHER YAH had been talking with my mom since I was a child. Later, when she was close to 40, she could discern the energy of a witch from a mile away, and she knew Nealie was one.

At the time, I was really still a stupid 40-year-old child, very naive. It amazes me now, when I think about traveling and moving around all my life with no fear, to realize just how naive I really was. Maybe that had something to do with why I never had any fear – or maybe it was the protection of YAHSHUA and the armor with which He covered me. I always felt Him and continued to pray every night, even when I dabbled in New Age practices. I didn't understand that I was mixing darkness with light. I was yet to discover that it doesn't work.

While I was in Boston, Nealie took me to Salem, to what she called "a white witches gathering" to do a rain dance for the state of

Texas, which was having a drought. We spent the morning making head wreaths with flowers and ribbons to match our flowery dresses. In my naive mind, I was dressing for who I had in my heart, that being FATHER ELOHYM (GOD). Three days after we participated in this dance, it rained in Texas! Wow. This was cool, I thought.

Then Nealie took me into a book store and loaded me up with pagan books, spending a small fortune for a mound of books. I put them on shelves and hardly touched most of them, but I read enough to learn a lot of things that helped clarify my choice in coming back full circle to YAHUWAH, our CREATOR. (I burned them all while in San Miguel Allende, my next stop.)

By this time I was working with leather designs. For years I had bought my leather in the Boston area, so all I had to do was call and make an order and have it shipped to my mom's. When I visited, I would load up and take it back to Mexico in my luggage. I really didn't know anything about Customs and legalities at that time.

Right after Nealie broke with my brother, he ended up in the hospital after trying to kill himself. After he got out of the hospital, I got a letter from Nealie, stating that she had sold her house and wanted to come to Mexico to see me and open an orphanage. That sounded cool. I asked how I could help.

The orphanage story was what she told me, and I, not yet having had my eyes open to the dark spirit realm, trusted her.

I asked Nealie to bring my leather down with her. Unfortunately, on her way to Cabo San Lucas from Boston, they stopped her in Customs in Mexico City. I was surprised when she stayed for three days and nights with the immigration officer in Mexico City. He helped her get the leather through customs, despite not having the right paperwork. Little did I understand back then, that FATHER is always in control. His lessons, as He guides us, are the raw material for molding us – the clay pots.

It wasn't long before Nealie had me tripping through the witch markets in Mexico, looking for herbs and candles to burn on full moons and/or on the first day of the Bible months. Everything was counterfeit and opposite to our FATHER'S times and ways. It was twisted, but at the time, I didn't recognize it as a clue to the presence of evil.

Nealie set up an appointment with someone on the mainland of Mexico. Putting it all together years later, I realized this was a male witch who was to help her with "eating my soul." Remember, Nealie didn't like my mom because my mother belonged to YAH. She had tried to get my brother to kill himself, but my mom's prayers were all over that. When that failed, I truly believe that she decided to come after me. I found out years later that she died from some sort of blood cancer shortly after she returned to America. I believe she had been after my blood to perform some sort of evil ritual to cure herself of the cancer.

But back to the story. Nealie finally got to Cabo San Lucas and bought airline tickets for the two of us to go to Cancun, via Mexico City, where she had planned to meet up with her new friend. She told me she had a meeting to discuss opening the orphanage and that I would be bored, so she would have a taxi take me to a pyramid site that was being excavated outside of Mexico City for some sight-seeing. Now I truly believe that she was really meeting with a male witch to discuss my demise.

The pyramid site was a big old site that was in shambles back then. I went to the top of a hill and sat and meditated on the beautiful day. I was the only person there for hours. When I opened my eyes, I had a vision of a wedding dance going on below. It reminded me of the pagan dance we did for the Texas rain. The women in the vision were dressed in plain flowy dresses with flowers in their hair. Strange music was being played with odd instruments.

Then, in the vision, I turned towards the mountains behind me and on my left side, I saw where these people lived. They lived in cave-like structures dug into the mountains. There were ladders made from vine-ropes for climbing up to their spaces.

Still in the vision, I got up and walked over to an ancient room made of stone. It had a large statue in front of the opening and reminded me of the outside of Egyptian temples. It was a giant structure. Like a rock cave, it was square on the outside, but inside, I saw a small rounded room. As I stepped onto the threshold to enter, a strong wind of energy pushed me out of it. Thinking this was just the wind, I tried again to step back into the entrance to the room. Again a very strong energy pushed me out and would not let me enter. I closed my eyes for understanding of what could be going on.

What I saw in my mind's eye was a dark-skinned, native Indian man with feathers in his hair and bands around his wrists. With a large strand of jade beads around his neck, he definitely was some sort of warrior or priest. He was sitting open-legged on the dirt floor. In front of him was a hole in the dirt, dug into the middle of the room. He was holding a big heart in his hands that was still pumping. I saw drops of blood coming off of this heart as his hand hovered over this hole with the blood dripping into it. (What I was seeing had nothing to do with drugs because I was no longer using or doing any kind of drugs in my life.)

My vision was interrupted by a sense of an earthly presence. As I turned, I could see down the hill that I had climbed, where a few workmen were starting to come up the hill. I assumed they were excavating. I told them about the cave people living in the mountain sides, using rope ladders to get to their homes. I thought it would help them to know where to excavate.

These visions did not seem strange or out of the ordinary for me. From the time I was very young, I was able to see beyond temporal realms to see what I called "angel beings of light." Whatever it was that I was feeling now was very strong. When I was young, I thought everyone could see what I saw, but I learned as I grew, that very few could see beyond the veil or the natural realm or whatever it was I was experiencing. I always called on angels when I needed help and they were always there. It was normal for me to call on Gabriel and Michael to cover me in light. With my inner vision, I could see a very large angel hovering around, protecting me.

I heard a car horn and went down the small mountain to find Nealie and her friend at the bottom.

Before we left Mexico City, Nealie dragged me to the witches' (bruah) markets, gathering herbs that she could not get in the USA to do whatever she was doing. I was baffled trying to understand witches and herbs. What did I know? Nothing.

In prayer, I felt I was always to have a candle lit in the hotel rooms while I was with Nealie. Calling on YAHSHUA (Greek for JESUS) most every night before I laid my head down to sleep, and thanking Him for the protection with which He surrounded me, was the one stable part of my world.

The next morning, we left by plane for the Yucatan and started our journey south in the mainland of Mexico. Nealie always took taxis, saying a woman should never walk alone. She made reservations at the best hotels and the best restaurants. On this trip we were always surrounded by festive music, drinks and great food. She paid for everything. It didn't take long before she found a very young musician, a Peruvian flute player, to hang with. He played the same kind of strange music that I had heard being played near the pyramid at the wedding of the people of the past that I had envisioned. She was always trying to fix me up with someone, but I had no interest. I just wanted to get back into quiet time with YAHSHUA.

Now, many years later, as I put all the pieces together, I believe Nealie had it planned to meet with the main big guy male witch to perform a ceremony that involved trading my soul for her health.

Little did I know at the time, that she was sick and dying with a blood illness. She was going to use me to deal with it. I believe she was bidding for my soul in her efforts to extinguish the light that my family (seed) line carried forward. I don't really know for sure, but over the years putting the pieces together, I think that was her plan.

Nealie and I spent about six weeks waiting for the appointment with the male witch. While she waited, she played with her flute player – drinking, dancing and totally immersed in a lifestyle that I didn't even like. It was keeping me from prayer and my writing. I missed my private time with ELOHYM, CREATOR of all.

Hiding her intentions with the male witch, Nealie told me she was waiting to meet with someone about how to develop an orphanage in Mexico, and I believed her. I have to laugh at how naive I was back then. Thankfully, I was protected by YAHSHUA, but I was spiritually asleep.

We stopped at all the pyramids that had been excavated by that time, hiring private taxis to drive us to and from the most elaborate hotels deep in the jungles. It was amazing that they were even there. In those days, we could climb on the pyramids, and there were all kinds of artifacts just scattered and lying around with no one to question or bother us. It was just us and the private driver. It was really amazing – very primitive back then with no paved roads to the temples; just dirt roads.

Finally, the time came for Nealie to say goodbye to her flute-playing friend and meet with the man she had brought us all the way from Cabo to the Yucatan to meet. That day she took me to buy black candles and bought me a red garnet bracelet which she put on my wrist.

We met the man at a big restaurant and had some drinks and dinner. Then she talked with him in mumbled words, as if the conversation was in a tunnel. I couldn't make the words out. She pointed to the garnet bracelet that she had earlier put on my wrist. I heard her telling the man that the garnets had to do with blood. As she drew her hand closer to my wrist with the bracelet on it, the bracelet fell off, right into her hand. What was that??? We all laughed. She fastened the clasp of the bracelet back onto my wrist and we ate. Thinking of this now, I wonder if this was part of the magic ceremony she was to have while having sex with this man, in exchanging my pure blood for hers??? or perhaps something to do with defiling it???

We went by taxi to His apartment building. She had bought a fresh-cut red rose, and gave it to me, telling me she was going upstairs with this man to talk about orphanage stuff. I was to sleep downstairs, right under their room. It was just rooms like a hotel, with no kitchen. Nealie and this male witch were right above me, burning black candles.

If I got scared as I laid down to sleep, I was supposed to call out her name while holding the rose she'd given me.

In this dark room where I was alone, in nowhere land on a secluded dark street, I started to see figures on the walls. They were shadows of short, dark figures that looked like midget men, tip-toeing across the walls. I started to pray, holding the rose and calling on YAHSHUA (I called Him "JESUS" back then). It was a night of heavy warfare. What that meant, I had no idea back then. All I knew was that all night I had to cling to YAHSHUA and fight the demon that (I guess) was supposed to kill me.

By the time dawn came, I was exhausted. I heard something rattling the door handle. Nealie used a key to come into the room. When she saw me sitting there, she got madder than a bull in a china closet. She had the man-witch call for a cab, aggressively pushed me into it, and had the driver drive us to a very small hotel, the Blue Parrot, on the beach. It had three small, bamboo cabins back then. Now it's a big hotel and restaurant in Playa del Carmen.

What a ride. I was basically sick and worn out. Her plan was broken, and I was still, for the most part, oblivious to the details of everything that was happening.

Nealie said she was banishing me (a pagan thing) from our friendship, so we flew back to Cabo San Lucas. I knew I had to get her out of the small town where we both now lived. I told her she had to leave this town. Not long after that, she left Cabo, and then died back in the Boston area.

I believe that because FATHER can see past, present, and future, He knows who belongs to Him from the beginning of time. He knows who will choose Him, and who He can mark as His chosen. He sees this before we do, and gifts us with the faith we need to hold us and strengthen us through our coming-home days. This is my opinion and may be far from His truth; I don't know for sure.

My heart cries with deep sobs at times, thinking of the miracles and blessings He has given me, and continues to give. I don't deserve any of this, and sometime I cry from shame, knowing how much I definitely don't deserve any of His blessings and protection.

I pray that people will listen and wake up while there is still time. ABBA is calling us back to Himself and is using signs to show us what is happening and what is coming. He molds us to do His work when we make the Bondsman commitment to Him. (A bond-servant choses to serve his or her master for life without complaint, going where he or she is called to go, or doing whatever the master requires.)

The Bible says the last days will be "as in the days of Noah." I can see that the ancient gods are being released back to Earth to make one last, fierce effort to steal every soul possible.

The Blood Bank

When a very dear acquaintance in Cabo almost died, friends called on me to do whatever I could. At the time, I was using healing powers and had become known to some as a healer. Were these powers from FATHER? According to my present understanding, while I was not yet walking in the light of true understanding of Him and of His Word, FATHER will use us in whatever way will help us with our decisions further down the road. I may be wrong, but I believe I was being trained and groomed to serve Him in an authentic way, during those early days.

Because of my friend's near-death experience, I was led to build a blood bank in Cabo. The nearest hospital that would possibly have blood was over two-and-a-half hours away by car. In an emergency, when one needed blood, it was not available in Cabo in those days.

I had heard about a person who had bled to death because there was no blood available locally. He had gone out fishing on a large boat and caught a very large marlin. When he reeled it in and landed it in the fishing boat, during the struggle to get it off the hook, the fish's bill cut the man almost in half. By the time the man got to land, he had lost a massive amount of blood, but there was no help for him.

After hearing about this tragedy, and with a friend almost dying, I knew I needed to pray on it and find out if ABBA wanted me to do something. The result was that on October 13th, 1987, He answered my prayers by leading me to help support the establishment of a blood bank in Cabo. I ran an advertisement in the Cabo newspaper, asking people to get in touch with me if they were interested in giving blood, whenever it might be needed, to help build a blood bank for Cabo. The interest and support was out there.

I started collecting names, blood types, phone numbers, addresses, and people's sex sleeping habits (because we were deep into the AIDS pandemic). I kept the info in a file on index cards.

October 20th 1987, just seven days after I had lit a candle in hope of setting this up, FATHER'S help showed up in an amazing way. That morning, I went to have coffee at a little coffee shop.

I saw a man walk into the cafe. He had just gotten off the ferry. We got chatting and he shared that he really had no idea why he was in Cabo St. Lucas. His wife wasn't with him because he was looking for a job and would send for her when he got established. He said he had a calling to come to Cabo, from across the sea, to find work. It still amazes me how FATHER works. It turned out that this man was a qualified blood technician! I immediately set him up with a doctor for a meeting in town. The subject for discussion would be the solution to the problems I had asked Father to solve.

When the Father is involved in our lives, the truth is stranger and more amazing than fiction. It just gets stranger, and more wonderful, as the years go by.

CHAPTER 6

San Miguel Allende

Bringing Me Back From Drunk to His Glory

One night, while I was still in Cabo San Lucas, I dreamt all night long that I was searching for the Mexican town of San Miguel Allende. In my dreams, I studied map after map, over and over again, to find this town to which I knew YAHSHUA was leading me. It was amazing. I knew He was getting me ready for my next step in life. I was always grateful to have, and love, my CREATOR GOD to whom I could pray through the Name of YAHSHUA, and who I knew would direct my path.

I left Cabo after going to breakfast by myself on my 40th birthday, November 12, 1987. After breakfast, I paid the tab and took a taxi to the airport. I hopped on a plane to the mainland, and was off to find out where I was being sent.

That night of dreaming led to a 37-year span in San Miguel Allende (so far). It has not all been roses, but some of the thorns

YAHSHUA has allowed have been used to help me see roses. I hope this last move here takes me right on into His eternal Kingdom. I surely hope and pray that wherever He takes me next, it will be even nearer to Him, closer than in prayer, so close that I can hear his breathing next to me. YAHSHUA our King.

How does one explain experience after experience of either rejoicing in His absolute glory – or crying out for His strength to wade through the darkness back into the light? It was a process of transitioning from the state of the first Adam (carnal humanity) to life in the second Adam (CHRIST our Savior).

I am going to sum up this last 37 years as best as I can. San Miguel Allende is where I truly became one with YAHSHUA, and was finally able to enter fully into the process of casting off the things of the world that were holding me back. I came to understand that I am a bond-servant to CHRIST and I want to serve as part of His army here on planet Earth. So many are waking up to the reality of His loving plan for our lives, whether it may be sitting in prayer or planting seeds for those who may find and use them when they most need them.

I arrived in San Miguel a semi-drunk, searching for GOD in all the wrong places. I was hanging with the wrong crowd, smoking grass every day and unknowingly dancing to the worldly music of the devil. I did (and still do) pray almost every night, unless I was so drunk that I just passed out; but no matter my condition, I always felt the presence and protection of the HOLY SPIRIT around me.

The fact that my Godly mom would sit us children in front of the TV watching Bible stories when we were growing up, was an incredible gift, because it gave us a foundation for our lives. It was enough to introduce me to the knowledge of YAHSHUA JESUS and give me a life-long hunger to know Him more.

What I didn't have was the *whole* truth. All I had were bits and pieces that I had read and heard throughout my life. I needed the full understanding of His way, His story – the one He left for us in His book, the *Bible*.

Now it was time for me to learn about *repentance* and my need for it as a grown woman.

I had some understanding of spiritual warfare and the battle between the kingdom of darkness and the kingdom of light, because by now I had actually seen demons in people when YAHUWAH used me to rebuke them in His Name – as he did with Armandingo – but I still had much to learn.

Even as I write these words, I am beginning to understand more about my spiritual filth – dirty rags – things I have never realized before. For me, repentance is a life-long journey of rejecting everything that separates us from GOD. That's why it's so important to read His Word and pray to learn His ways. How can anyone understand what they need to repent for if they don't know FATHER'S ways?

It's hard to take an honest look at who you have been. My heart cries in shame when I think of the things I did and the way I lived. It grieves me to think I could do this to my loving FATHER who always has a plan. His plan for me was to look deeply at my remaining demons while pulling the story of my life together to write this book. He wanted me to be a witness of His glory for my readers, but also to grow closer to Him in the process of writing. I can't be more grateful and I'm humbled to think He has a place for me in His Kingdoms. (Note: There is the Kingdom of EL (GOD) which is within us; and the Kingdom coming to Earth, which is CHRIST'S Kingdom. Right now we live in Satan's earth kingdom. For those interested in deeper understanding, this is another area of study.)

An Angel Delivering Dene's Name

My son was born January 2nd, 1989.

At the age of 41, I had a son out of wedlock. When I was pregnant, an angel came to me in a vision, giving me the name of my one and only child. His name was to be "Dene."

When Dene was about 14-months-old, we were at a friend's house for dinner. Dene got into a drawer and opened a small bottle of pills, swallowing 11 very small, strong, Halcion tranquilizers.

As we rushed him to the emergency room, I was frantic. Two doctors arrived. I followed them into the small operating room as they started working on my son. All I could do was drop to my knees in a corner and pray. Suddenly, I was touched on the shoulder and given an inner knowing that he would live. I'll never forget that touch, because immediately, the adrenaline and fear left my body. My fear had been real, but a touch from the hand of eternal love replaced it. I turned to see who had touched me, but there was no one in the room except the two doctors who were pumping Dene's stomach.

Another time, I took Dene for his vaccinations. I wasn't keen on them because there were so many more than there used to be when I was growing up. Back then, only one or two were required. I felt as though I was between a rock and a hard place, because vaccines had become the law. No vaccines, no school – even in Mexico. So I took him.

Huge mistake. Right after we got home, Dene started crying and running a very high fever. It lasted for three days. He cried around the clock with hardly any sleep. Nevertheless, the nurses had no concern and assured me that the reaction would pass.

After the vaccination, Dene stopped walking and started crawling again. He did not start talking until he was three-years-old.

Another Vision of Mary

In a vision, I saw a staff being given to me by CHRIST. In this vision, it seemed that the Virgin Mary was to put a crown on me, but as she stepped up in front of me with the crown of jewels, CHRIST stepped in front of her, handing me a staff. I could see a flash of light on the very tip of it as He handed it to me.

These visions strengthened my faith in YAHSHUA and assured me of the truth of His Word, but I started to question why the Catholics worshiped the Virgin Mary. Remembering the picture of her in the Catholic schoolyard, I began to wonder what it really was they were worshiping.

One time as I drove home saying the rosary, I saw the Virgin of the rosary standing in front of me. As I drove, I could see her standing against the blue of the sky with the rosary in her hand. At that time, I felt that she guided me safely on my 13-hour drive home.

But why was I praying to a Virgin and not directly to GOD (the FATHER, SON and HOLY SPIRIT)? Nowhere in FATHER'S Word does it tell us to pray to Miriam, YAHSHUA's birth-mother, or to "Mary," as her name has been translated.

Jeremiah 7:18 mentions the "queen of Heaven," but it's in the context of provoking GOD (FATHER) to anger. *"The children gather wood, the fathers kindle fire, and the women knead dough, to make cakes for the queen of Heaven. And they pour out drink offerings to other gods, to provoke me to anger."* Does this say Mary is another god (a little "g" god)? What is this about?

Jeremiah 44:19 again mentions the "queen of Heaven," but this time it's within the context of not having the approval of their husbands. *"And the women said, 'When we made offerings to the queen of Heaven and poured out drink offerings to her, was it without our husbands' approval that we made cakes for her bearing her image and poured out drink offerings to her?'"*

Jeremiah 44:16,17 clearly shows the reference to the "queen of Heaven" as being within the context of the rebellion of the people against Jeremiah. *"As for the Word that you have spoken to us in the name of the Lord, we will not listen to you. But we will do ev-*

erything that we have vowed, make offerings to the queen of Heaven..."

I began to question things like why my mother and her sister shunned the rosaries I made for them. Being a jeweler, I was making rosaries and Virgin jewelry, thinking it was the right thing to do – until I had an eye-opening understanding of who the Catholics were really worshiping. Now I understood that the pagan statues in the giant Catholic churches had different names on them before being replaced with "Mary, Mother of JESUS," not even acknowledging "Miriam" as the true birth name of YAHSHUA's mother.

Names have meaning. According to Isaiah 26:4, the Name of GOD is "YAHUWAH" (YAH). As I previously mentioned, from that Name of GOD, we take the MESSIAH's name to be YAHSHUA, which means "YAH is Salvation." "EMMANUEL" means "GOD with us." It is a descriptive name or title, while YAHSHUA is His given name. It is the name the angel Gabriel told Joseph to name Mary's child: *"You are to give Him the name "YAHSHUA," because He will save His people from their sins"* (Matthew 1:21). So "YAHSHUA," (translated from EMMANUEL) means "Salvation."

The name, "JESUS," has no meaning in Hebrew. Originally

"IESOUS," "J" replaced "I" in English in the late 1800's. It is the translation from Hebrew to Greek, but it is actually the Greek form of "Joshua," which was a common Jewish name.

YAHSHUA was a mid-eastern Hebrew man. He was certainly not an American.

I was beginning to wake up from the same dead sleep that is immobilizing a great many people right now as we get closer to the coming of our true King of Kings, YAHSHUA.

Along the path of my journey, I discovered the Commandments of YAH, as given in the original Hebrew – and the Saturday Shabbat (the seventh-day Sabbath) as the intended day of rest and worshiping our CREATOR (instead of Constantine's Sunday). In the fourth century, the dates and times were changed to suit Constantine's agenda, and the Feasts of the Lord (YAHUWAH'S appointed times for meeting with Him) were outlawed. Sunday, the day most Christians observe as the Sabbath, became man's appointed time – but it was never FATHER'S appointed time. So much has been changed through the centuries to shift our faith from the ways of the anointed CHRIST. Scripture warns against changing His times and days.

As I read the Word of ELOHYM, I was awakened to recognizing the Kingdom of GOD as reality. It was an amazing merging of dimensions. The Kingdom of GOD is *now* within us...and yet it is *coming* after the 1000 year millennium of CHRIST.

Father's Money

One day I found myself out of money and unable to pay the next month's rent, and so I packed up Dene and put all the things I had been blessed in making, buying and reselling into the car. Off we went to Houston, where I had an appointment with a possible client. By the time we got to the hotel, I had one dime and a maxed-out credit card left to my name.

It was getting dark and I was on my way to the hotel when Dene started shouting, "Donaldssss. I want Donaldssss!" He had noticed a MacDonalds playground from the back seat. At that time, Dene was about three-years-old and just starting to talk. Back then, a Happy Meal was 28 cents. To him, it would have meant not only food, but a chance to play in the playland. Sadly, my last dime was not going to cover it. I got Dene into bed, rocked him to sleep and began to go to war with FATHER ELOHYM.

With no help from Dene's biological father, I took the matter up with my ABBA FATHER. I reminded Him how I was always in prayer and had faith and it didn't make sense how I was always worried about how, and from where, the money for food and rent would come. In my need, it was a pretty intense time of warfare prayer.

That night, in my sleep, I heard, "All money is MY money and all you have to do is ask."

I gather that FATHER put me on His gift list, because the next day I went to my 9 a.m. appointment and sold $2000.00 worth of my creations – in US dollars – the largest amount I had ever sold to one store at one time. How anyone can not worship and obey our grand, loving, caring FATHER is beyond my understanding.

Ever since that time, I have never again had to worry about money to pay for anything I need. I haven't necessarily had a lot of extra, but I've always had enough to pay for my needs.

My work has been seen and loved by many people. After that, I was able to open five show rooms across the USA. It wasn't long before I was doing shows in Paris and Dubai. My business was booming. I opened a store in San Miguel Allende.

Through it all, I honored my FATHER and remembered the Sabbaths. I made it known that I was always closed on Saturdays. Even when I did shows, my booth was closed on Saturdays to honor

His appointed time. In those situations I would pay for my spot in the show, but I was not there so I could be with my ELOHYM, CREATOR of all. I truly believe He has taken care of me because I gladly want to be with Him and never expect anything in return for loving Him. I can't make it without His Grace.

Cleansing the House

I was shaken awake one night around three a.m. I jumped out of bed with an overwhelming realization that the pieces of so-called "art" I'd been naively using as decorations were actually demonic idols. I was horrified.

I had a beautiful collection of original oil paintings of the Virgin Mary and JESUS hanging all over my home – right next to the life-size Buddhist statues, the life-size statue of the Virgin Mary, and the vintage statue of JESUS that I had purchased from an antique store. I had been told that it had been used by the Catholics to parade around town and had been brought over from Spain, hundreds of years before.

I stood staring at my museum of idols and wondered, "What the hell have I been doing?" I quickly took a knife to the paintings, cutting them from their frames and rolling them up into one giant roll. I turned over the statues and dragged them out into the yard. Then I took the devil folk art masks off the walls, crashed the folk art statues and pulled everything into the yard for a big bonfire.

Crushing statues of dragons with a sledge hammer in my yard, I carried the chunks into the pot holes in the street, filling them so cars could crush them into powder. The Word of ELOHYM is very clear that we are to have no idols, no pictures of idols, no carved figures or stone gods. I don't even want to tell you what I did to the acrylic Virgin that I had purchased at a church auction.

Since that night, I have never said another rosary or prayed to the Virgin. I hacked up a life-size, wooden statue of Buddha to use as firewood for the bonfire. Anyone who would criticize this cleansing of my home has not read the true Word of our CREATOR. I cry in shame at my ignorance of spiritual realities and the instructions given to us by YAH.

Scripture warns that GOD'S people can perish from lack of knowledge. It is so important that we read and understand His Word so that we will know what's happening and where we are on the timeline of YAHUWAH'S plan. Only then can we be free of fear and walk in the ways of YAHSHUA, allowing Him to carry us.

That morning I went into my store and took every piece of jewelry that was virginized (new word meaning styled after the idolization of Mary) and destroyed them all. I was not making idols for anyone, anymore, ever. Amen.

Once again I began to see visions. They had become rare while I was dancing to the worldly beat.

Vision of an Armored Soldier

In one of my visions, I saw a person in a full set of solid silver amor, sitting on top of a beautiful, big white horse. Around the edges of his helmet, I could see a neatly combed, bobbed hairdo. The features were those of a light-skinned person. I couldn't tell if it was a male or a female, but I felt it was me. As I watched, I saw something coming at this person. It was coming from far away in the Heavens, spinning around and around until it finally stopped and stood straight up. It was a glorious, large, silver, two-edged sword that came to rest standing right in front of me. I can't explain it. I hope it was a picture of me returning with YAHSHUA when He returns to take His people home.

My Repentance

Around 2010, Dene was diagnosed with schizophrenia, having had several other such diagnoses in earlier years. This brought me to my knees – again. I called on FATHER as often as I could.

As I sat in prayer one day, I had an open-eyed vision. I saw CHRIST sitting in the same place that my body was sitting. Then, I saw myself kneeling by His side, with my head in His lap, but not touching His body. He had his right hand just inches above my back, not touching me. He was consoling me as I wept deeply, emptying my soul of the darkness I had encountered over the years.

I was completely still in a space of eternal love, as He gave me such deep compassion that it emptied my soul of all the pain of so many dark happenings in my lifetime. All the New Age beliefs, the witchcraft, the false religions, the idol worship, and everything that had exalted itself above YAHSHUA was torn down in my soul.

Receiving the Torah in my Heart

On Passover, 2014, I went out of the house after reading one of the books of the Torah. It was the first time I had read the whole book of Deuteronomy from beging to end. I had been cooking a lamb chop and there were some blood drippings in a pan. Taking the pan outside, I spread the blood over the front metal doors of the yard and over the corners of the inside doors with some small branches. Then, with black paint, I wrote the names "ELOHYM YAHUWAH."

After I was finished, as I turned to go back inside the house, I started to see a vision. I saw three crosses up on a hill. The sky was reddish black. I thought of YAHSHUA. Then I saw scrolls; more and more and more scrolls being downloaded, one after another, in my mind. What was happening? I truly had no idea at the time, and waited until it finished. Then I went on into my home, and started praying.

More Possessions

During this time, Dene was in and out of detox centers. Did it do any good? That's a big question. The doctors put him on medications which he threw away as soon as he was released. I believe the medications worked for a time only because the demons that had been hanging around Dene's soul stayed away because they were bored being stuck around a locked up body that was no fun. I also believe this was why Dene stopped taking the medications. He was under the influence of dark spirits. He was always talking to things I couldn't see.

FATHER allowed me to see demons that He wanted me to see, but not all. When I saw dark spirits, it was in FATHER'S timing, not mine. Everything happens in his time.

By now, I was spending most of my time in deep study of Scripture. For the first time, I started studying under different teachers on YouTube. I was learning Scripture in a way that opened up realms of wisdom and understanding like never before. Line by line, here a little, there a little, I soaked up knowledge.

The visions I had had before this, finally started to make sense. It was like being given a wedding band from YAHSHUA my Savior. The vision of the double-edged sword, the warrior sitting in armor and the warfare through which I'd been struggling – and so much more – were like gifts that had been given to me but needed explanation. The understanding was all in the written Bible. It was amazing to me that the visions were now starting to make sense.

I had never known anything about the Bride of CHRIST or the Sword being the Word of ELOHYM. YAHUWAH had been preparing me for this time, the end of the sixth day, after 6000 years of the history of the world.

To the FATHER, one year is as 1000 years to us. He created His world in six days and on the seventh day He rested. We will rest in His Kingdom with His SON (BEN YAHSHUA) throughout the last thousand year millennium. Our eternal bodies of light will replace our earthly bodies as though they were unwanted rags.

I was learning what was given to us children of the one true ELOHYM YAHUWAH. He was (and is) shaking me awake, bringing me back to His Torah to learn how to walk the true walk, one step at a time.

Around 2017, I broke my back falling off a ladder, and was blessed to spend three months in bed with the Bible while I healed.

During that time, the spiritual warfare was fierce, because the enemy did not want me to learn the true Word of GOD.

Three Dark Angels

Three demons got into my head, probably having entered through some part of my life that I had not yet fully submitted to GOD. These were the hardest I'd ever had to fight, and they lingered the longest. After almost six weeks of calling on FATHER'S help, I was sent a messenger, or an angel, to help get them out of my mind and send them back to wherever they had come from.

Daniel was a homeless man who had simply shown up out of nowhere. I never imagined him to be a helper, but I took pity on him and got a room for him in the hotel where I was staying. The experience became not only supernatural, but hair-raising to the extent that the hotel had to call in a hazmat team to clean the room where he had stayed. They then boarded it up. When Daniel left, so did the demons that had had a hold on me. Did they leave me and attach themselves to him? It would take another whole book just to tell about the grace I was given throughout this experience.

After that experience, I was given the ability to see bulgy-eyed, swampy-looking, creepy demons in people. At times, ABBA would use me to rebuke them in His Name; not all the time, but randomly, on His terms.

From this time, I have never strayed away from the RUACH. I can actually feel Him at work in me, especially when I'm in deep prayer.

The blessings FATHER has given me are so numerous, it's impossible to remember every one. Even the particularly hard times were blessings because they were allowed in my life to make me stronger and bring me to my knees in understanding. I have no idea at times why FATHER would be so gracious as to give me to CHRIST, to hold in His hands all my life.

I am overwhelmed at the glory with which He has blessed me. My heart is filled with gratitude and shame at the same time; shame because I don't deserve His mercy…and yet FATHER loves me.

Now I always pray directly to ABBA FATHER in YAHSHUA's Name. Like a loving father, He always shows up; sometimes right away and sometimes in response to my persistence. He needs to hear us knocking and calling and knocking and calling.

The "RUACH" is the blessed HOLY SPIRIT of our CREATOR YAHUWAH. As we show YAHUWAH our love, and demonstrate our obedience to His instructions, He grants us space with Him. We enter into His presence through our faith and experience of Him as we move forward in life. We are children of the light, being guided back to our CREATOR FATHER.

The Battle

There is a battle going on and one must be strong enough in our FATHER'S presence to resist and overcome other spirits that seek to attach themselves to us. Becoming stronger through prayer with YAHUWAH every morning and night is a must, in order to be attuned enough to even understand that the danger exists. One must love Him with every cell, and want to walk in Him, giving Him total control. Most people have no idea of the battle for their souls that is taking place within them.

I am not saying one must acknowledge these things to be graced into His Kingdom. I don't know what His terms are for others. He judges the hearts of people and we all have different paths to walk. I think being a disciple or a bond servant involves a walk so close to Him in a quest to know Him more, that one can feel His SON is walking this walk within us.

We need to be perfected in order to stand in front of Him. This could take a lifetime – and might take another 1,000 years with the new Millennium coming soon.

In this new Millennium, I believe we will be given a gift of guidance as a loving father gives to his sons and daughters. Some of us will receive this guidance sooner than others, working as priests, teachers and kings to help guide others in this up-coming Millennium of time. I don't know about you, but this is the job I would like, being as close to YAHSHUA's presence as possible when He returns – even closer than when we are in deep prayer time. Yes, this job I desire, with all my wanting, Amen.

I Heard, "Write the book, 'Witness Me'"

I was 76-years-old, and in prayer for hours one night, when I received a message from the Most High. He told me to open a Bible school, and I heard Him say, "Write the book, 'Witness Me.'" A few days after hearing this instruction, I started questioning myself. Did He really ask that, or was I dreaming? I was truly questioning my sanity.

After about a week or so, I opened a drawer and, sitting right on top of everything else in the drawer, was an old hard-copy of a book that I had begun to rough-out, but had not touched for years. I had never noticed it sitting there before, and had totally forgotten that I even still had it. It had been the furthest thing from my mind for close to 40 years.

You can't make this up. What I heard, clearer than the sounding of a bell, was that the SPIRIT was telling me, "Yes, write it." Consequently, this book is my witness of how incredibly great GOD has been throughout my life; even before I was delivered from darkness, false teaching, and Satan's attempts to take my soul. My greatest joy now, is communicating with my Savior in amazing realms of prayer, walking with Him within my heart.

What I love about the RUACH is that He is always with me. Anyone who is listening, will hear the nudging. I love it when I talk about Him to others and He fills me with a breath of energy that makes every hair on my body stand up. I think He loves it when I talk about Him.

CHAPTER 7

Suffer the Little Children

I believe the following experience was given to me because it may help others who have children of their own, or they may know people who have been victims of the evil crime of pedophilia that is rampant around the world in these dark times. As previously mentioned, I believe the evil spirits of pedophilia make way for dark spirits to live in the bodies of victims. Pedophilia involves not only the violation of the victim's body, but the raping of his or her soul through evil sexual perversion. Perversion has always been here, but people are waking up to this evil, because the light of justice is exposing it so that we can take a bolder stand against it.

During this time of my life, I had an encounter with a young adult who had been molested as an infant. I believe that when a child is molested at such a young age, the mind often splits and allows another spirit to take over the body. After seeing this boy's eyes turn totally black as he talked about shooting heroin to see Satan, I knew I needed lots of prayer time to be able to deal with the situation.

I spent the night in deep prayer, asking for help, and was granted the grace of FATHER to use His Word in prayer to release the demons that had been stealing the life force of this child.

As I prayed, envisioning the Blood of YAHSHUA covering this child, the air around became full of demons flying around him. I could see their dark shadows. I just kept praying.

They started talking to each other. One said, "Do you know who that is?"

Another one said, "No, it's not from our realm."

When it said that, I knew I had angelic help fighting through me for the boy's soul. These foul spirits recognized the greater power of YAHSHUA coming against them from the realm of light, dispelling their darkness.

When the child started to cry, I knew he was free. He wept and wept and allowed the HOLY SPIRIT to wash him clean. The demons couldn't stay where the Blood was being applied and the Name of YAHSHUA was proclaimed.

In situations like this, one must be equipped for doing warfare and understand the need for prayer. There must be assurance that the battle is spiritual and belongs to ABBA FATHER.

In this situation, because the child did not receive the Blood of CHRIST, the demons soon returned for another bout of warfare. This time, I was shown in prayer what was needed to release the demons and close the portal. Since that time, this child has not been possessed, but has been plagued with strongholds as he struggles to recuperate from a lifetime of being plagued by these entities. Lots of love and understanding is needed through this difficult period. Most of the children victimized by pedophiles have no idea what is happening and need to be brought into the light and acceptance of the Blood of our one and only Savior, YAHSHUA.

Little ones are suffering abuse all around us in these dark days. Parents and care-givers need to know what they're dealing with and how to help their children.

This battle for the souls of our children is not a battle that can be fought in courts or through therapists. It's a spiritual battle fought in realms beyond our own.

The only way to fight this battle is to overcome the darkness with the light of YAHSHUA. We have to take the authority He gives us through His Name, His Word and His Blood. When we stand in that authority, evil has to flee because YAHSHUA is greater, but our standing has to be with full authority. We can't go up against strong demonic forces with pathetic little bits of relationship with YAHSHUA; the only way to overcome is by being filled with the HOLY SPIRIT who will do the fighting for us.

If one is not strong enough, one must search for FATHER'S helpers. Many are now receiving the power of the RUACH (HOLY SPIRIT) to battle the darkness. Sadly, most churches are not given instructions for fighting spiritual warfare. It is left to individuals to find revivals where people are gaining strength in FATHER'S Word, the Sword of the SPIRIT. Only by getting a child who has been abused to YAHSHUA, is there hope for restoration and deliverance from evil, or the child will return to torment. It is the only way to find freedom.

When sexual abuse happens to a child, even if the body is not taken over by these entities right away, the area in the brain dealing with sexuality is prematurely activated and there is consequent damage to the brain. In many (probably most) cases, the trauma becomes an open door for demon spirits to enter, even at a future time, and live through the host body.

Knowing the Enemy

The Book of Enoch reveals what these demons are, where they

came from and how they function in our world. Briefly, when the rebellious angels of Genesis, Chapter Six, (the fallen angels - also called Nephalim) came down to Earth and had sex with human women, their offspring were giants. These were the Rephaim. They were part human and part divine. They were hybrid humans, composed of hybrid body, hybrid soul and carnal spirit. While their fathers loved them and wanted them to enjoy the heaven they remembered, GOD refused to offer salvation to them because they were hybrid; they were not what He created. Consequently, the realm of darkness is filled with lost demon spirits of these Rephaim and Nephalim who do the bidding of Satan.

FATHER sent the great flood because He had to destroy hybrid humanity. Everyone had been infected by the interference of the Nephalim and humans were no longer what FATHER created. Only Noah's family had pure human blood, and so they were preserved in the Ark to restart the human race.

When the hybrid-human Rephaim die, their spirits live on because they have eternal souls. These disconnected spirits have to find bodies through which to live and carry out their evil deeds. Wherever they can find open doors (entrances made legal through misalignment with ELOHYM), they enter and function through that person or animal. They will also fasten themselves to objects that are misaligned with GOD; like ungodly books, paintings, carvings Ouija boards or even things like mirrors, as I came to find out.

When a child is abused, the trauma imposed by a predator becomes a legal portal into the human soul, because it is misaligned with GOD. As such, the trauma becomes a legal entry point for a demon looking for a host body. One must be strong through the Blood of our Savior.

Living in Christ

Life is a process. People sometimes slide backwards and fall back into the grip of Satan. It is at those times when we have to pray that God will have vessels to work through to rescue them – perhaps again and again. But we don't give up, because we have witnessed His grace, glory and victory over the dark realm.

Without YAH, mothers can do nothing substantial for their abused children because it is the spirits that have entered them at the time of trauma that cause all the discord and darkness in their lives. With YAH, all things are possible, because His light dispels the darkness. It is His power, working through us, that sets our children free to love and worship Him.

Epilogue

And so, here we are, at the end of this book. I could go on and on with more, but this is it for now.

I heard it said that if the disciples of CHRIST had written down every miracle that YAHSHUA did, the world couldn't hold all the books. It would take another whole span of time for me to adequately appreciate what YAHSHUA has done for me. It is impossible for me to feel sufficient gratitude towards Him for loving me so much that He chose me, despite all my faults. It just amazes me.

I have always been grateful to YAHSHUA (JESUS), the anointed MESSIAH, for His caring heart towards me. Every time I have been in need, YAHSHUA has been there for me – and you will find He's there for you, too, if you just open your heart and ask Him to fill your spirit.

I often not only see His face and the light around YAHSHUA, but I can feel the love of His presence. My desire to be pure love burns inside of me. The flame of the Comforter, or HOLY SPIRIT (RUACH), takes me to the height of pure love in a dying world. Amen.

TEPHILLAH AZARYAHU (PRAYER OF AZARIAH)

The Prayer of Azariah and Song of the Three Holy Children, abbreviated "Pr Azar," is a passage which appears after Daniel 3:23 in some translations of the Bible, including the ancient Greek Septuagint.

1 And they walked in the midst of the fire, praising ELOHIYM, and blessing YAHUAH.

2 Then Azaryahu stood up, and prayed on this manner; and opening his mouth in the midst of the fire said,

3 Blessed are you, O YAHUAH ELOHIYM of our fathers: your name is worthy to be praised and glorified forevermore:

4 For you are righteous in all the things that you have done to us: yea, true are all your works, your ways are right, and all your judgments truth.

5 In all the things that you have brought upon us, and upon the holy city of our fathers, even Yerushalayim, you have executed true judgment: for according to truth and judgment did you bring all these things upon us because of our sins.

6 For we have sinned and committed iniquity, departing from you.

7 In all things have we trespassed, and not obeyed your commandments, nor kept them, neither done as you have commanded us, that it might go well with us.

8 Wherefore all that you have brought upon us, and everything that you have done to us, you have done in true judgment.

9 And you did deliver us into the hands of Torahless enemies, most hateful forsakers of ELOHIYM, and to an unjust king, and the most wicked in all the world.

10 And now we cannot open our mouths, we are become a shame and reproach to your servants; and to them that worship you.

11 Yet deliver us not up wholly, for your name's sake, neither disannul your covenant:

12 And cause not your mercy to depart from us, for your beloved Avraham's sake, for your servant Yitschaq's sake, and for your holy Yashar'el's sake;

13 To whom you have spoken and promised, that you would multiply their seed as the stars of heaven, and as the sand that lies upon the seashore.

14 For we, O YAHUAH, are become less than any nation, and be kept under this day in all the world because of our sins.

15 Neither is there at this time prince, or prophet, or leader, or burnt offering, or sacrifice, or oblation, or incense, or place to sacrifice before you, and to find mercy.

16 Nevertheless in a contrite heart and a humble RUACH let us be accepted.

17 Like as in the burnt offerings of rams and bullocks, and like as in ten thousands of fat lambs: so let our sacrifice be in your sight this day, and grant that we may wholly go after you: for they shall not be confounded that put their trust in you.

18 And now we follow you with all our heart, we fear you, and seek your face.

19 Put us not to shame: but deal with us after your lovingkindness, and according to the multitude of your mercies.

20 Deliver us also according to your marvellous works, and give glory to your name, O YAHUAH: and let all them that do your servants hurt be ashamed;

21 And let them be confounded in all their power and might, and let their strength be broken;

22 And let them know that you are ELOHIYM, the only ELOHIYM, and glorious over the whole world.

23 And the king's servants, that put them in, ceased not to make the oven hot with rosin, pitch, tow, and small wood;

24 So that the flame streamed forth above the furnace forty and nine cubits.

25 And it passed through, and burned those Kasdiym it found about the furnace.

26 But the angel of YAHUAH came down into the oven together with Azaryahu and his fellows, and smote the flame of the fire out of the oven;

27 And made the midst of the furnace as it had been a moist whistling wind, so that the fire touched them not at all, neither hurt nor troubled them.

28 Then the three, as out of one mouth, praised, glorified, and blessed, ELOHIYM in the furnace, saying,

29 Blessed are you, O YAHUAH ELOHIYM of our fathers: and to be praised and exalted above all forever.

30 And blessed is your glorious and holy name: and to be praised and exalted above all forever.

31 Blessed are you in the Temple of your holy glory: and to be praised and glorified above all forever.

32 Blessed are you that behold the depths, and sit upon the Keruviym: and to be praised and exalted above all forever.

33 Blessed are you on the glorious throne of your Kingdom: and to be praised and glorified above all forever.

34 Blessed are you in the expanse of heaven: and above all to be praised and glorified forever.

35 O all ye works of YAHUAH, bless ye YAHUAH: praise and exalt him above all forever,

36 O ye heavens, bless ye YAHUAH: praise and exalt him above all forever.

37 O ye angels of YAHUAH, bless ye YAHUAH: praise and exalt him above all forever.

38 O all ye waters that be above the heaven, bless ye YAHUAH: praise and exalt him above all forever.

39 O all ye powers of YAHUAH, bless ye YAHUAH: praise and exalt him above all forever.

40 O ye sun and moon, bless ye YAHUAH: praise and exalt him above all forever.

41 O ye stars of heaven, bless ye YAHUAH: praise and exalt him above all forever.

42 O every shower and dew, bless ye YAHUAH: praise and exalt him above all forever.

43 O all ye winds, bless ye YAHUAH: praise and exalt him above all forever,

44 O ye fire and heat, bless ye YAHUAH: praise and exalt him above all forever.

45 O ye winter and summer, bless ye YAHUAH: praise and exalt him above all forever.

46 O ye dews and storms of snow, bless ye YAHUAH: praise and exalt him above all forever.

47 O ye nights and days, bless ye YAHUAH: bless and exalt him above all forever.

48 O ye light and darkness, bless ye YAHUAH: praise and exalt him above all forever.

49 O ye ice and cold, bless ye YAHUAH: praise and exalt him above all forever.

50 O ye frost and snow, bless ye YAHUAH: praise and exalt him above all forever.

43 O all ye winds, bless ye YAHUAH: praise and exalt him above all forever,

44 O ye fire and heat, bless ye YAHUAH: praise and exalt him above all forever.

45 O ye winter and summer, bless ye YAHUAH: praise and exalt him above all forever.

46 O ye dews and storms of snow, bless ye YAHUAH: praise and exalt him above all forever.

47 O ye nights and days, bless ye YAHUAH: bless and exalt him above all forever.

48 O ye light and darkness, bless ye YAHUAH: praise and exalt him above all forever.

49 O ye ice and cold, bless ye YAHUAH: praise and exalt him above all forever.

50 O ye frost and snow, bless ye YAHUAH: praise and exalt him above all forever.

51 O ye lightnings and clouds, bless ye YAHUAH: praise and exalt him above all forever.

52 O let the earth bless YAHUAH: praise and exalt him above all forever.

53 O ye mountains and little hills, bless ye YAHUAH: praise and exalt him above all forever.

54 O all ye things that grow in the earth, bless ye YAHUAH: praise and exalt him above all forever.

55 O ye mountains, bless ye YAHUAH: Praise and exalt him above all forever.

56 O ye seas and rivers, bless ye YAHUAH: praise and exalt him above all forever.

57 O ye sea monsters, and all that move in the waters, bless ye YAHUAH: praise and exalt him above all forever.

58 O all ye fowls of the air, bless ye YAHUAH: praise and exalt him above all forever.

59 O all ye beasts and cattle, bless ye YAHUAH: praise and exalt him above all forever.

60 O ye children of men, bless ye YAHUAH: praise and exalt him above all forever.

61 O Yashar'el, bless ye YAHUAH: praise and exalt him above all forever.

62 O ye priests of YAHUAH, bless ye YAHUAH: praise and exalt him above all forever.

63 O ye servants of YAHUAH, bless ye YAHUAH: praise and exalt him above all forever.

64 O ye RUACHoth and souls of the righteous, bless ye YAHUAH: praise and exalt him above all forever.

65 O ye holy and humble men of heart, bless ye YAHUAH: praise and exalt him above all forever.

66 O Chananyahu, Azaryahu, and Miysha'el, bless ye YAHUAH: praise and exalt him above all forever: for he has delivered us from She'ol, and saved us from the hand of death, and delivered us out of the midst of the furnace and burning flame: even out of the midst of the fire has he delivered us.

67 O give thanks unto YAHUAH, because he is gracious: for his mercy endures forever.

68 O all ye that worship YAHUAH, bless the ELOHIYM of elohiym, praise him, and give him thanks: for his mercy endures forever.

Notes

Notes

www.ingramcontent.com/pod-product-compliance
Lightning Source LLC
Chambersburg PA
CBHW040108100526
44584CB00029BA/3939